Little Muslims Inspiration Series

Fatima Al-Fihri

The founder of the world's first university

Dedicated to
My biggest inspirations,
My wonderful children

Written by
Maryam Yousaf

Illustrated by
Sheeba Shaikh

Published by
Muslima Today Kids

This is the story of a young Muslim girl named Fatima Al-Fihri. Fatima was a kind-hearted girl, and the daughter of a wealthy businessman called Mohammad Al-Fihri.

The family was so rich that they were like royals.

Fatima had a sister called Mariam.

Their father loved them both very much. He made sure that they got only the best in education. They were deeply loved and cared for by their father.

Fatima and Mariam had a fantastic Muslim upbringing.
They loved to pray and read the Qur'an.
They also loved to learn.

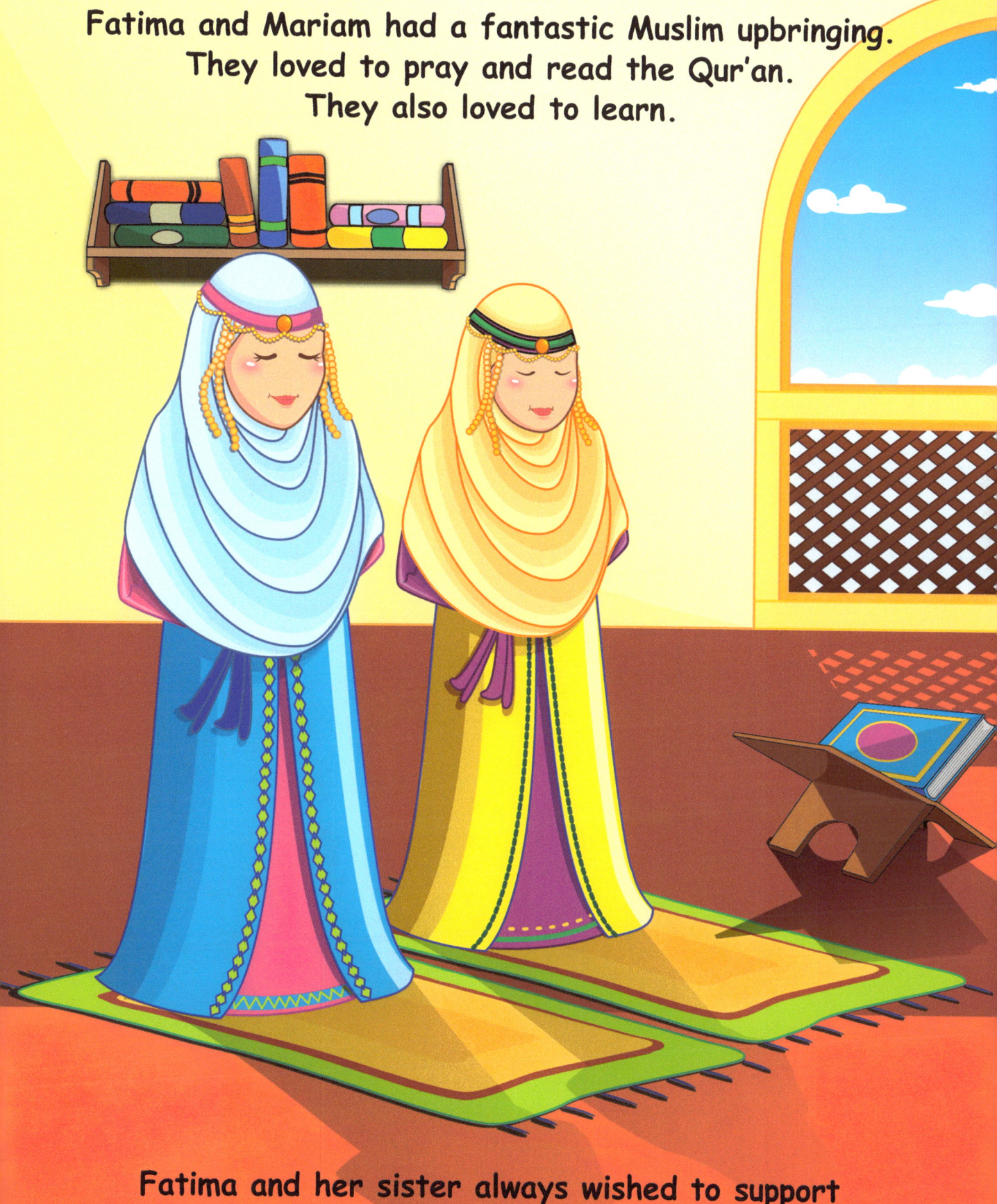

Fatima and her sister always wished to support
Islamic education. This was their dream.

Fatima lived with her family in Tunisia. But one day, her father decided it was time for them to move to Morocco, to a city called Fez.

Sadly, some time later,
Fatima's husband and father both passed away.

Innā lillāhi wa innā ilayhi rāji'ūn
Surely, to Allah we belong, and to Him we return.

Fatima and Mariam were now left with a huge sum of money from their father's wealth.

They realised that they had the power to do a lot of good for their community.

So they began to think of ways in which they could help others.

Fatima and Mariam had an idea that people at that time thought was quite strange.

They decided to build a mosque where people could come to pray and gain Islamic knowledge.

This was their chance to make their lifelong dream come true.

Fatima spent all of her inheritance in building a mosque called Al-Qarāwiyyīn. She named the mosque after her birth-city in Tunisia.

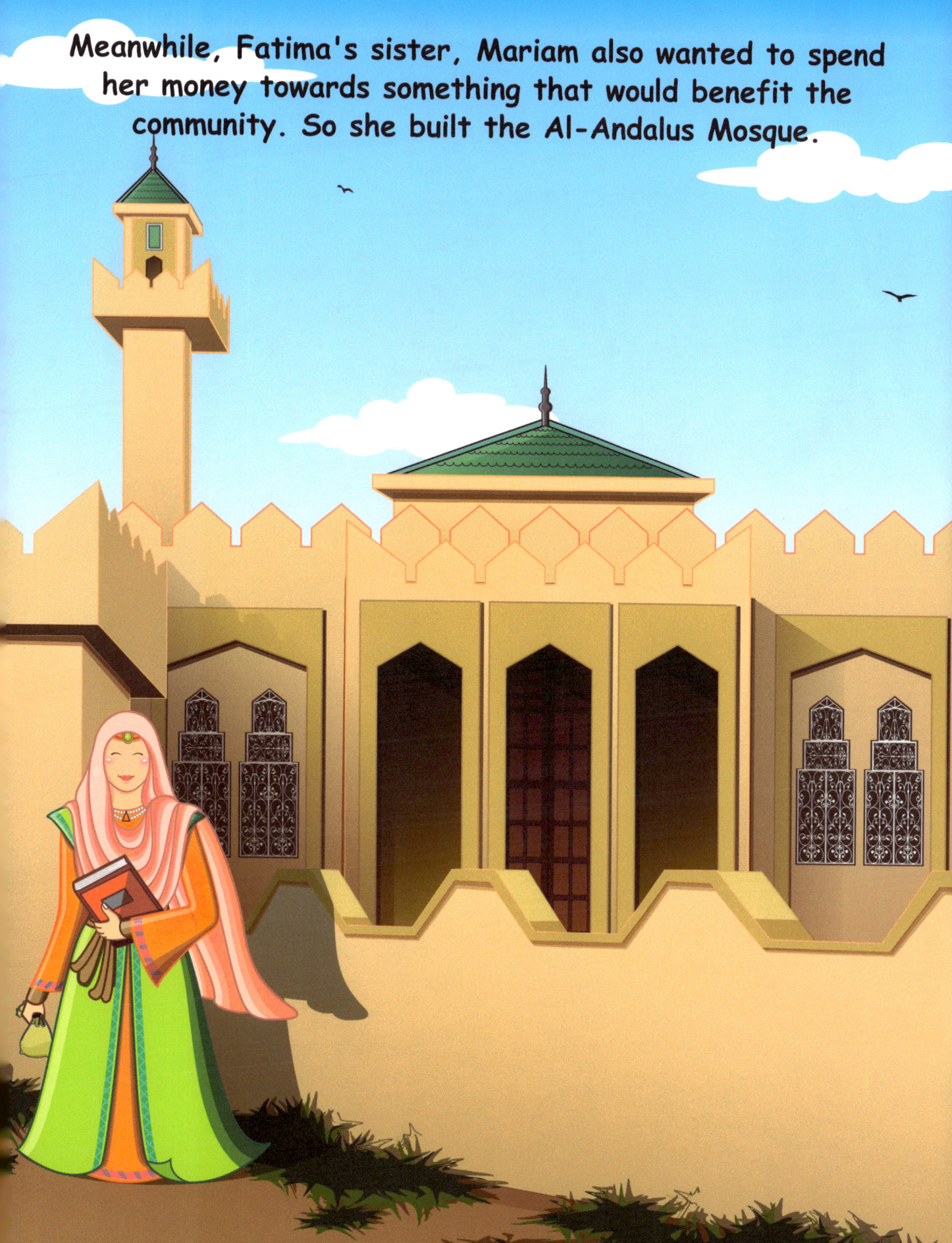

When the final brick was put in the mosque, the first thing Fatima did was pray two units (raka'āt) of prayer (salāh) to express her thankfulness to Allah for answering her prayers and making her dream come true.

The mosque grew bigger and bigger until it became one of the largest universities in the whole world.

Al-Qarāwiyyīn is now considered to be the oldest university in the world. It is still one of the greatest landmarks of the country, and continues to encourage learning and education even today.

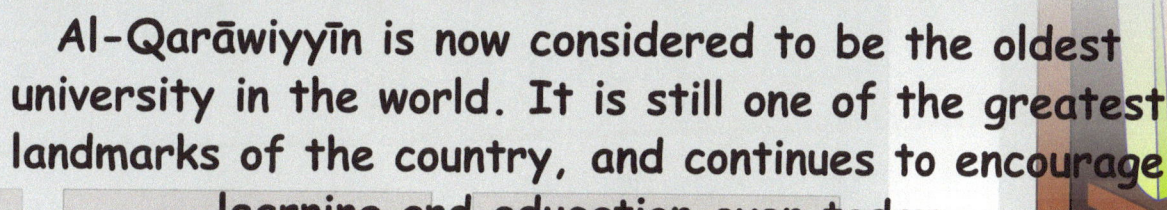

The founder of this magnificent university was none other than Fatima Al-Fihri – a Muslim woman with a dream and determination to teach and inspire learners all over the world.

MORAL

What we discover from Fatima's story:

Sincerity and acts of goodness always pay off.

If you really want something, then increase in good deeds such as giving charity or fasting for the pleasure of Allah.

No matter your circumstances, never give up. Even though Fatima lost her father and her husband, she never lost hope. She did everything in her power to make the world around her a better place.

Always be kind and think of others. Fatima had inherited a large amount from her father. But she didn't greedily keep it all to herself. Instead she shared her wealth with her community and left a great legacy behind her.

Always believe in yourself. Even though Fatima's idea was quite strange for that time, she believed in herself, despite what people thought.

Just like Fatima, with great focus, prayer and determination you too can accomplish anything.

First published in 2017 by **Muslima Today Kids**
www.muslimatoday.com

Edited by
Umm Marwan Ibrahim

Text and illustrations copyright © by Maryam Yousaf

All rights reserved. No part of this publication may be reproduced in any form or by any electronic or mechanical means including photocopying, recording, and information storage and retrieval systems.

Muslima Today
www.muslimatoday.com
ISBN 978-0-9934078-5-7

www.ingramcontent.com/pod-product-compliance
Lightning Source LLC
Chambersburg PA
CBHW042131040426
42450CB00003B/148